D1326073

# Christmas Present,
# Christmas Past

## from you to me®

**from you to me®**

concept by Helen Stephens
and Neil Coxon

# *Christmas Present, Christmas Past*

## *from you to me*®

This journal is for you to capture and share the magic of your Christmas.

Year after year this decoration can be updated with your precious memories and photographs telling the tale of what you did for the festive celebrations and describing your hopes for the year ahead.

This will become one of your own Christmas traditions . . . creating a story that will be treasured forever.

*This Christmas journal belongs to*

A bit about myself . . .

`

# *Christmas Present, Christmas Past*

*Year* _____

# *Christmas Eve*

Where we were . . .

Who was there . . .

Some of the conversations we had . . .

What we were excited about . . .

Things that made the evening memorable . . .

We went to bed at . . .

# *Christmas Day*

We woke up at . . .

Where we celebrated . . .

Who was there . . .

What we did . . .




Traditions we followed and/or started . . .

# *Christmas Day*

Some of the memorable presents that were
given and received . . .

What we ate and drank . . .

# *Christmas Day*

Things that made this Christmas special . . .

Things that made us laugh and smile . . .

What was going on in the wider world?

# *Reflections and Aspirations*

The best moments of the past year . . .

Hopes and wishes for the future . . .

Plans for the coming year . . .

Some of the 'new year' resolutions set . . .

# *Christmas Present, Christmas Past*

## *Year* _____

# *Christmas Eve*

Where we were . . .

Who was there . . .

Some of the conversations we had . . .

What we were excited about . . .

Things that made the evening memorable . . .

We went to bed at . . .

# *Christmas Day*

We woke up at . . .

Where we celebrated . . .

Who was there . . .

What we did . . .



Traditions we followed and/or started . . .

# *Christmas Day*

Some of the memorable presents that were
given and received . . .

What we ate and drank . . .

## *Christmas Day*

Things that made this Christmas special . . .




Things that made us laugh and smile . . .

# What was going on in the wider world?

# *Reflections and Aspirations*

The best moments of the past year . . .

Hopes and wishes for the future . . .

Plans for the coming year . . .

Some of the 'new year' resolutions set . . .

# *Christmas Present,*
# *Christmas Past*

*Year* _____

## *Christmas Eve*

Where we were . . .

Who was there . . .

Some of the conversations we had . . .

What we were excited about . . .

Things that made the evening memorable . . .

We went to bed at . . .

# *Christmas Day*

We woke up at . . .

Where we celebrated . . .

Who was there . . .

What we did . . .

Traditions we followed and/or started . . .

# Christmas Day

Some of the memorable presents that were given and received . . .

What we ate and drank . . .

# *Christmas Day*

Things that made this Christmas special . . .

Things that made us laugh and smile . . .

# What was going on in the wider world?

# *Reflections and Aspirations*

The best moments of the past year . . .

Hopes and wishes for the future . . .

Plans for the coming year . . .

Some of the 'new year' resolutions set . . .

# *Christmas Present, Christmas Past*

*Year _____*

## *Christmas Eve*

Where we were . . .

Who was there . . .

Some of the conversations we had . . .

What we were excited about . . .


Things that made the evening memorable . . .


We went to bed at . . .

# *Christmas Day*

We woke up at . . .

Where we celebrated . . .

Who was there . . .

What we did . . .

Traditions we followed and/or started . . .

# *Christmas Day*

Some of the memorable presents that were given and received . . .

# What we ate and drank . . .

# *Christmas Day*

Things that made this Christmas special . . .

Things that made us laugh and smile . . .

What was going on in the wider world?

# *Reflections and Aspirations*

The best moments of the past year . . .

Hopes and wishes for the future . . .

Plans for the coming year . . .

Some of the 'new year' resolutions set . . .

# *Christmas Present, Christmas Past*

*Year* _____

# *Christmas Eve*

Where we were . . .

Who was there . . .

Some of the conversations we had . . .

What we were excited about . . .

Things that made the evening memorable . . .

We went to bed at . . .

# *Christmas Day*

We woke up at . . .

Where we celebrated . . .

Who was there . . .

What we did . . .


Traditions we followed and/or started . . .

# *Christmas Day*

Some of the memorable presents that were
given and received . . .

What we ate and drank . . .

# *Christmas Day*

Things that made this Christmas special . . .

Things that made us laugh and smile . . .

What was going on in the wider world?

# *Reflections and Aspirations*

The best moments of the past year . . .

Hopes and wishes for the future . . .

Plans for the coming year . . .

Some of the 'new year' resolutions set . . .

# *Christmas Present, Christmas Past*

*Year* _____

## *Christmas Eve*

Where we were . . .

Who was there . . .

Some of the conversations we had . . .

What we were excited about . . .

Things that made the evening memorable . . .

We went to bed at . . .

# *Christmas Day*

We woke up at . . .

Where we celebrated . . .

Who was there . . .

What we did . . .

Traditions we followed and/or started . . .

# *Christmas Day*

Some of the memorable presents that were given and received . . .

# What we ate and drank . . .

# *Christmas Day*

Things that made this Christmas special . . .

Things that made us laugh and smile . . .

# What was going on in the wider world?

# *Reflections and Aspirations*

The best moments of the past year . . .

Hopes and wishes for the future . . .

Plans for the coming year . . .

Some of the 'new year' resolutions set . . .

# *Christmas Present, Christmas Past*

*Year* _____

# *Christmas Eve*

Where we were . . .

Who was there . . .

Some of the conversations we had . . .

What we were excited about . . .

Things that made the evening memorable . . .

We went to bed at . . .

## *Christmas Day*

We woke up at . . .

Where we celebrated . . .

Who was there . . .

What we did . . .



Traditions we followed and/or started . . .

# *Christmas Day*

Some of the memorable presents that were
given and received . . .

What we ate and drank . . .

# *Christmas Day*

Things that made this Christmas special . . .

Things that made us laugh and smile . . .

# What was going on in the wider world?

## Reflections and Aspirations

The best moments of the past year . . .

Hopes and wishes for the future . . .

Plans for the coming year . . .

Some of the 'new year' resolutions set . . .

# *Christmas Present, Christmas Past*

*Year* _____

# *Christmas Eve*

Where we were . . .

Who was there . . .

Some of the conversations we had . . .

What we were excited about . . .

Things that made the evening memorable . . .

We went to bed at . . .

# *Christmas Day*

We woke up at . . .

Where we celebrated . . .

Who was there . . .

What we did . . .

Traditions we followed and/or started . . .

# *Christmas Day*

Some of the memorable presents that were
given and received . . .

What we ate and drank . . .

# *Christmas Day*

Things that made this Christmas special . . .

Things that made us laugh and smile . . .

What was going on in the wider world?

## *Reflections and Aspirations*

The best moments of the past year . . .

Hopes and wishes for the future . . .

Plans for the coming year . . .

Some of the 'new year' resolutions set . . .

# *Christmas Present, Christmas Past*

*Year* _____

# *Christmas Eve*

Where we were . . .

Who was there . . .

Some of the conversations we had . . .

What we were excited about . . .

Things that made the evening memorable . . .

We went to bed at . . .

# *Christmas Day*

We woke up at . . .

Where we celebrated . . .

Who was there . . .

What we did . . .




Traditions we followed and/or started . . .

# Christmas Day

Some of the memorable presents that were given and received . . .

# What we ate and drank . . .

# *Christmas Day*

Things that made this Christmas special . . .

Things that made us laugh and smile . . .

What was going on in the wider world?

## *Reflections and Aspirations*

The best moments of the past year . . .

Hopes and wishes for the future . . .

Plans for the coming year . . .

Some of the 'new year' resolutions set . . .

# *Christmas Present, Christmas Past*

*Year* _____

## *Christmas Eve*

Where we were . . .

Who was there . . .

Some of the conversations we had . . .

What we were excited about . . .

Things that made the evening memorable . . .

We went to bed at . . .

# *Christmas Day*

We woke up at . . .

Where we celebrated . . .

Who was there . . .

What we did . . .

Traditions we followed and/or started . . .

# *Christmas Day*

Some of the memorable presents that were given and received . . .

What we ate and drank . . .

# *Christmas Day*

Things that made this Christmas special . . .

Things that made us laugh and smile . . .

What was going on in the wider world?

# *Reflections and Aspirations*

The best moments of the past year . . .

Hopes and wishes for the future . . .

Plans for the coming year . . .

Some of the 'new year' resolutions set . . .